DESERTS

ENDANGERED
BIOMES

DONNA LATHAM

Nomad Press
A division of Nomad Communications
10 9 8 7 6 5 4 3 2 1
Copyright © 2010 by Nomad Press

Printed by Regal Printing Limited in China,
June 2010, Job Number 1005019
ISBN: 978-1-934670-86-6

Questions regarding the ordering of this book should be addressed to
Independent Publishers Group
814 N. Franklin St.
Chicago, IL 60610
www.ipgbook.com

Nomad Press
2456 Christian St.
White River Junction, VT 05001
www.nomadpress.net

Image Credits

corbisimages.com/ Walter Bibikow, cover; James Hardy, i.

©iStockphoto.com/ Jan Rysavy, 1; Jussi Santaniemi, 1; Tobias Helbig, 3; Christine Glade, 3; ziggymaj, 4; Tobias Helbig, 5; Jan Will, 7; Klaas Lingbeek, 8; Konstantin Nestruev, 9; Miroslav Tolimir, 9; Hsing-Wen Hsu, 9; KingWu, 10; Brandon Jennings, 11; Suzannah Skelton, 12; Kate Payton, 12; Dmitry Kutlayev, 12; Eric Isselée, 13; Steven Love, 13; Thomas Dam, 14; Maximilian Allen, 14; Matt Cooper, 15; Dave Rodriguez, 15, 22; Alexander Hafemann, 16, 23; Nicholas Roemmelt, 17; Guillermo Perales, 18; Kate Leigh, 18; kavram, 19; Mark Coffey, 20; Erik Seo, 21; Deanna Quinton Larson, 22; Anna Utekhina, 24; Domenico Pellegriti, 26; Tina Rencelj, 27.

CONTENTS

What Is a Biome?

Grab your backpack! You're about to embark on an exciting expedition to explore one of the earth's major **biomes**: the desert!

A biome is a large natural area with a distinctive **climate** and **geology**. The rainforest is a biome. The tundra in the Arctic is a biome. So is the desert.

Did You Know?

Scientists don't agree on how many biomes there are. Some divide the earth into five biomes. Others argue for 12.

Words to Know

biome: a large natural area with a distinctive climate, geology, and set of water resources. A biome's plants and animals are adapted for life there.

climate: average weather patterns in an area over a period of many years.

geology: the rocks, minerals, and physical structure of an area.

adapt: changes a plant or animal makes to survive in new or different conditions.

ecosystem: a community of living and nonliving things and their environment. Living things are plants, animals, and insects. Nonliving things are soil, rocks, and water.

environment: everything in nature, living and nonliving.

Biomes are the earth's communities. Each biome has its own biodiversity, which is the range of living things **adapted** for life there. It also contains many **ecosystems**. In an ecosystem, living and nonliving things interact with their **environment**.

Teamwork keeps the system balanced and working. Earth's biomes are connected together, creating a vast web of life.

2

Landscape and Climate

The desert is the most **arid** biome. We think of deserts as hot places filled with sand dunes and blowing sand. But deserts can be rocky too, with deep canyons and stony mountains. Some deserts stretch across vast gravel **plains**. Other deserts are even solid ice!

Did You Know?

What's the hottest temperature ever recorded? In 1922, the thermometer soared to 136 degrees Fahrenheit (58 degrees Celsius) in the Sahara Desert.

of the Desert

About one-fifth or 20 percent of our planet's surface is desert. You'll find deserts on almost every continent. Maybe you've heard of the Sahara Desert in northern Africa, the Gobi Desert in Mongolia, or the Kalahari Desert in southern Africa. Maybe you've even visited the Mojave Desert in the southwestern United States.

Words to Know

arid: very dry, receiving little rain.

plains: large, flat land area.

Daily temperatures can range from a scorching 110 degrees Fahrenheit (37 degrees Celsius) during the day to a frigid 30 degrees Fahrenheit (-1 degree Celsius) at night.

Why do temperatures in the desert nose-dive so drastically? Desert air is extremely dry. Because the air contains so little moisture, it can't hold the heat. When the sun sets, temperatures plummet.

5

The Sahara Desert is the largest desert in the world. It is about the size of the United States.

Here: Deserts are very dry and get less than 10 inches of rain in an entire year.

There: Rainforests get 79 inches or more of rain each year.

It doesn't rain in the desert very often, but when it does rain, the landscape of some deserts explode into vibrant life. Temporary ponds spring up during heavy rainfall. Then they dry up and vanish. Before ponds disappear, though, plants and animals take full advantage of them.

Antarctica is the planet's coldest, driest, most blustery place. You wouldn't expect it to be a desert. But it is. It's a cold desert wrapped in a permanent ice sheet.

An oasis is a place in a desert where underground water rises up to the surface. Even in the middle of the desert there are areas where brilliant green plants grow, villages exist, and travelers can get water.

Word Exploration

The word *oasis* comes from the Greek word meaning "dwelling place." Today the word has come to mean a retreat, or a place that gives relief from the troubles of the world.

Antarctica receives nearly the same amount of moisture each year as the Sahara Desert! How cold can a desert get? One July day in 1983, the temperature plunged to -129 degrees Fahrenheit (-89 degrees Celsius) in Vostok, Antarctica.

Plants Growing in the

In the extreme

environment of the desert, survival is tricky. Soil is coarse, rocky, and salty. Plants encounter frequent **droughts**.

The bristly Saguaro cactus has many **adaptations** to these harsh conditions. Its stems are pleated like accordions. When rain makes a rare appearance, the pleats puff up. They suck the water in, stash it away, and tap into the supply during droughts.

Words to Know

drought: a long period without rain.

adaptation: the development of physical or behavioral changes to survive in an environment.

transpiration: evaporation of water from plants. Evaporation is when water turns to water vapor and goes into the air.

Desert Have Adapted

The Saguaro cactus has a waxy coating on its skin, which seals in moisture and cuts down on transpiration.

Did You Know?

Native Americans used the Joshua tree's sturdy leaves to weave baskets and shoes.

Meanwhile, Joshua trees use spiky, hairy leaves to protect themselves from the fierce sun and wind. These trees grow as high as 40 feet (12 meters). You can only find them in the Mojave Desert of Arizona, California, Nevada, and Utah.

In South Australia, the crimson Sturt's desert pea survives by using a vertical taproot. Rather than spreading out in shallow soil, the root plunges straight down, seeking out water from deep in the ground.

Animals Living in the

Animals survive in the dry, challenging environment of the desert with adaptations!

To avoid the sun's heat, animals hang out in shady areas around rocks and shrubs, or in cool burrows in the sand. Many animals are nocturnal, which means they scout around for food only at night.

What do the bilby of Australia, the jackrabbit of the American Southwest, and the fennec fox of Africa have in common?

These pint-sized creatures all have jumbo ears! Big ears radiate heat, allowing it to escape from the animals' bodies so they can keep cool.

Desert Have Adapted

Meanwhile, the leopard gecko (found in Iran, Iraq, and Pakistan) relies on its super-thick skin to keep from shriveling up like a prune in the dry desert. This insect eater uses its plump tail to store fat when food is scarce.

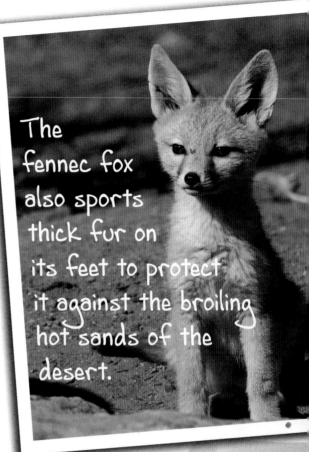

The fennec fox also sports thick fur on its feet to protect it against the broiling hot sands of the desert.

The Australian water-holding frog can live for nearly seven years on water held in its body. The frog burrows deep into the ground during droughts. It sheds layers of skin and uses them to cocoon itself. When a temporary pond develops, the frog devours its cocoon and travels to the surface of the water.

Roadrunners in the deserts of North America get water from their food.

Their long, slim bills hold snakes far from the roadrunner's body. Why? So angry snakes can't strike them. Two toes that face forward and two that point backward are perfect for dashing over sand to catch prey! These speedy birds can run 15 miles (24 kilometers) per hour.

Most desert animals are small, but there is one big animal that is built for survival in scorching heat. The camel!

What Eats What?

Roadrunners eat scorpions, lizards, and even deadly rattlesnakes. Lizards and scorpions eat insects while snakes eat lizards and other small animals that eat plants.

Long, curly eyelashes help bat away blowing sand.

Nicknamed "ships of the desert," camels are adapted for trekking over sand. Their humps weigh up to 80 pounds (36 kilograms) and act as storage tanks for fat to use when food grows scarce.

Camels have three sets of eyelids. The top set is thin and transparent. The camel snaps them shut during fierce sandstorms.

Environmental Threats

Climate change is making the desert the earth's fastest-growing biome. What happens in one biome can impact another. **Desertification** is when **fertile** land in other biomes turns into dry land. This creates more deserts.

Clearing land removes **vegetation** that protects soil from **erosion**. Desertification can happen when people clear land for crops.

desertification: when non-desert areas become desert.

fertile: land that is good for growing plants.

vegetation: all plant life in an area.

erosion: when land is worn away by wind or water.

overgraze: when animals eat plants faster than they can grow back.

Ranching also threatens other biomes and can turn them into deserts. When cattle **overgraze**, they gobble up all the plants. Grazing animals' hooves damage fragile soil and cause it to wear away.

18

Cactus collection threatens the desert. Visitors to the biome, thrilled by beautiful and exotic cacti, yank them out of the sandy soil and sneak them home. It's against the law. It often results in dead plants and endangers species.

19

Off roading is a pastime that many people enjoy. This is driving off-road vehicles in the desert. The vehicles leave tracks on the soil, which scars the land and kills off vegetation.

When vegetation dwindles in popular off roading areas, so does the animal population. Animals that hide in the sand can also be harmed. The sand viper, which hides so well in the soil, can become an accidental victim of off roading.

Biodiversity at Risk

Many plants and animals are endangered. And when an animal or plant **species** becomes extinct, that means it's gone forever. There are many causes of **extinction**. Natural occurrences, such as volcanic eruptions, have caused extinctions in the past.

Today, desert animals may become extinct when people overhunt them or when their **habitat** is damaged or destroyed.

Sometimes an **invasive species** disrupts the delicate balance of the local ecosystem. An invasive animal leaves less food for other animals to eat. An invasive plant leaves less resources for other plants.

Words to Know

species: a type of animal or plant.

extinction: the death of an entire species so that it no longer exists.

habitat: a plant or animal's home.

invasive species: a plant or animal species that enters an ecosystem and spreads quickly, harming the system's balance.

then: During the 1920s, there were 1,000 California desert tortoises per square mile in the Mojave Desert.

now: By 1990, the desert tortoise was listed as a threatened species. Human encroachment on the desert and cattle grazing on desert grasses destroyed much of the habitat of the desert tortoises. Disease introduced by captive tortoises released back into the wild put the population even more at risk.

23

Path to Extinction

Rare: Only a small number of the species is alive. Scientists are concerned about the future of the species.

Threatened: The species lives, but its numbers will likely continue to decline. It will probably become endangered.

Endangered: The species is in danger of extinction in the very near future.

Extinct in the Wild: Some members of the species live, but only in protected captivity and not out in the wild.

Extinct: The species has completely died out. It has disappeared from the planet.

The Future of the Desert

Deserts are growing all over the world.

Desertification is mostly caused by a growing human population that uses too much water. Grasslands bordering deserts are drying out from loss of vegetation and soil moisture. Clearing of land, ranching, plant collection, and off roading all destroy vegetation.

Since soil in the desert is held down by plant roots, once plants are destroyed the soil is too. The soil quickly erodes away in strong winds.

We have learned that what happens in one biome has an effect on other biomes as well. People are increasingly aware of the delicate balance of life on Earth. Many are devoted to conserving nature and preserving our biomes.

The desert is very fragile in many ways, because of the scarcity of water and plants. Most plants that live in the desert take a long time to grow. For example, the Saguaro cactus takes 200 years to grow to its full height of 30 feet (9 meters).

Conservation Challenge

Think about what You can do to help the desert environment. What actions can you take? How can you inspire others to do the same?

- Conserve water by taking showers instead of baths. Tubs take 70 gallons (265 liters) of water to fill, while showers use 25 gallons on average (95 liters). The amount of water you use in your shower depends, of course, on how long you spend there. So take shorter showers. Also, turn off the faucet while you brush your teeth. Why? Running the water for two minutes wastes two gallons of water. When you're done, make sure to turn the water all the way off so it doesn't drip all day.

- Purchase cacti at gardening and retail stores. Never take a cactus—or any plant—from its environment.

- Eat less meat. Cattle grazing on grasslands bordering the desert are a major cause of desertification. If everyone eats less meat we can slow this process.

- Treat the desert kindly. If you go to the desert, choose your activities carefully. Think about the impact you have on the desert.

Glossary

adapt: changes a plant or animal makes to survive in new or different conditions.

adaptation: the development of physical or behavioral changes to survive in an environment.

arid: very dry, receiving little rain.

biodiversity: the range of living things in an ecosystem.

biome: a large natural area with a distinctive climate, geology, and water resources. A biome's plants and animals are adapted for life there.

climate: average weather patterns in an area over a period of many years.

climate change: a change in the world's weather and climate.

desertification: when non-desert areas become desert.

drought: a long period without rain.

ecosystem: a community of living and nonliving things and their environment. Living things are plants, animals, and insects. Nonliving things are soil, rocks, and water.

environment: everything in nature, living and nonliving.

erosion: when land is worn away by wind or water.

extinction: the death of an entire species so that it no longer exists.

fertile: land that is good for growing plants.

geology: the rocks, minerals, and physical structure of an area.

habitat: a plant or animal's home.

invasive species: a plant or animal species that enters an ecosystem and spreads quickly, harming the system's balance.

overgraze: when animals eat plants faster than they can grow back.

plains: large, flat land area.

species: a type of animal or plant.

transpiration: evaporation of water from plants. Evaporation is when water turns to water vapor and goes into the air.

vegetation: all plant life in an area.

28

Further Investigations

Cherry, Lynn. *How We Know What We Know About Our Changing Climate: Scientists and Kids Explore Global Warming.* Dawn Publications, 2008.

Latham, Donna. *Amazing Biome Projects You Can Build Yourself.* Nomad Press, 2009.

Reilly, Kathleen M. *Planet Earth: 25 Environmental Projects You Can Build Yourself.* Nomad Press, 2008.

Rothschild, David. *Earth Matters: An Encyclopedia of Ecology.* DK Publishing, 2008.

Smithsonian Institution National Museum of Natural History
www.mnh.si.edu
Washington, D.C.

US National Parks www.us-parks.com

Enchanted Learning, Biomes
www.enchantedlearning.com/biomes

Energy Efficiency and Renewable Energy
www.eere.energy.gov/kids

Geography for Kids www.kidsgeo.com

Inch in a Pinch: Saving the Earth
www.inchinapinch.com

Kids Do Ecology
www.kids.nceas.ucsb.edu

Library ThinkQuest
www.thinkquest.org

National Geographic Kids
www.kids.nationalgeographic.com

NOAA for Kids
www.oceanservice.noaa.gov/kids

Oceans for Youth
www.oceansforyouth.org

The Nature Conservancy
www.nature.org

World Wildlife Federation
www.panda.org

Index